Glimpses of Indian Anthropology

(Social and Cultural Anthropological Studies in India)

Glimpses of Indian Anthropology

(Social and Cultural Anthropological Studies in India)

Biman Kumar Das Gupta

M.Sc. PhD.

AGAM

AGAM KALA PRAKASHAN

DELHI

First Published 2021

ISBN: 978-81-950098-9-3

Published by:
For **Agam Kala Prakashan**
34, Central Market, Ashok Vihar
Delhi - 110 052
Tel.: 91-11-27212195, 43513480
Fax: 91-11-27212195
Email: agamkala101@gmail.com, agambook@yahoo.com
www.agamkala.com

Composed by:
Sushil Kumar
Delhi - 110 052
Mobile: 9891395309

Printed in India

Contents

Preface 9

Chapter - I: The Beginning of Anthropology in India 11

Chapter - II: Some Important Research Studies Made 17

Chapter - III: India Shines: Western Scholars Visiting India 25

Chapter - IV: Indian Anthropology and the World 29

Chapter - V: Two Foreign Anthropologists and Indian Tribes 35

Chapter - VI: Important Researches Done in India: Phases 41

Chapter - VII: Social Movements 49

Chapter - VIII: Many Ethnographies studies and One Re-study 55

Chapter - IX: Author's involvement in Anthropological Projects 67

Chapter - X: Indian Tribes 79

Chapter - XI:	Indian enjoys Ethnic diversity of the land	85
Chapter - XII:	Epilogue	91
Appendix :	Other publications by the author	95
Index		97
Plates		103

Everyday

I

feel the blessings of my parents

Late Barun Chandra Das Gupta

Late Bani Das Gupta

and

I

seek the good wishes

of my deceased wife

Krishna

and

I also remember the

Compassionate guidance

of

Late Kamalesh Chandra Sen

who had a big role

in my higher studies

Preface

About ten decades ago, study of man, society and culture received priority in India. It was possible because of the opening of Post- Graduate studies in the University of Calcutta. Since then social and cultural Anthropologists in India and various institutes of the country initiated and completed a number of projects to accelerate the progress of the discipline. As a senior member, I was involved in many of these works..

My wife Krishna whom I lost in 2015, had liked that I should write about my experiences of and exposures with Anthropology and Anthropologists in India during the last six or seven decades .Later I have pondered and have felt that the idea can be translated into action. My son Basab Das Gupta and daughter-in-law Shyamasri Das Gupta, my daughter-Barnali Sengupta, Son-in-law Abhijit Sengupta, my grandsons Abhirup Sengupta and Anandarup Sengupta have always inspired me in this endeavour.

I am thankful to my friend Jayanta Kumar Sarkar, an Anthropologist of repute, for the suggestions made by him to improve the structure and content of the treatise.

I must thank Amitabha Sarkar and his wife Samira Das Gupta without whose help this publication would not have seen that light of the day. I am thankful to Shri, Debashis Biswas, EDP Section of Anthropological Survey of India for his painstaking help in typing of the manuscript. I also express thanks to the Publishing House-Agam Kala Prakashan, Delhi for their co-operation in publishing this book.

CHAPTER – I

The Beginning of Anthropology in India

The University of Calcutta started the Post Graduate course in Anthropology in 1920 and the first batch of students came out in 1922. Thus a new discipline of Anthropology started in India. The initiative was taken by Sir Ashutosh Mukherjee the then Vice-Chancellor of the University. The senate of the University adopted a resolution to start the Post-Graduate department of Anthropology. The resolution of the senate was forwarded to the Secretary, Department of Education; Government of India seeking government's approval. The resolution was readily approved making it possible to start the P.G. course from July 1920. Thus the first academic session 1920 – 1922 was an important milestone that marked the beginning of the study and research in the holistic study and understanding of man. In 1922 eight students came out successful; of them three got first class, three second class and two were place in the third class. Sisir Kumar Har stood first class in the first batch of successful candidates in 1922. Therefore, we can remember the name of Sisir Kumar Har as the first student who stood first class first in Anthropology in India.[1]

II
Teachers, the Taught and the Journal

As the faculty of Anthropology was established in 1920, Rama Prasad Chanda was its first Lecturer-in-charge. He was a scholar of Ancient Indian history and culture. In 1921, Shri L.K.A. Iyer joined the faculty as Lecturer in-Charge. Iyer later authored the 'Tribes and Castes in Mysore'. The department of Anthropology, in that period, has a number of other eminent scholars, too, such as, Haran Chandra Chakladar (an eminent Sanskrit Scholar), Narayan Chandra Banerjee (a Historian), Tarak Chandra Das (Scholar in Ancient Indian History & Culture), K.P. Chattopadhyay (an Anthropologist), Nirmal Kumar Bose (an Anthropologist and Human Geographer), Dharani Sen (an authority in Prehistoric Archaeology) and T.C. Ray Chaudhuri (who taught Racial History. In 1926 Dr. B.S. Guha also joined the Faculty for a short period.

Of the above scholars, T. C. Das who came from the discipline of Ancient Indian History & Culture, painstakingly built up **a tradition of field research in cultural Anthropology**. He authored a book (an ethnographic account) on Purum Kuki group of S.E. Manipur (details already noted elsewhere) and this account drew the attention of eminent western scholars to review and establish the principles of prescriptive alliance and generalised exchange system). T.C. Das also taught 'Man, Society and Culture' at the Indian Institute of Social Welfare and Business Management (IISWBM) – a premier Business Management Institute of the city of Kolkata. In the list of reputed members of the Faculty, we find. K. P. Chattopadhyay who was a student of Prof. W H R Rivers of Cambridge University and.

Biroja Sankar Guha was a PhD from Harvard University. In 1931 at the request of J.H. Hutton (the then Census Commissioner).Guha prepared a report on Racial elements in Indian population –a report which became a part of 1931 census report of India. Guha later, as per Government of India's instruction, founded the Anthropological Survey of India and became its first Director.

III

Earliest Journals

In 1921, an '*Anthropology Club*' was established with Tarak Chandra Roy Choudhury as its founder Secretary. It was a forum for academic discussion and lectures. For some time the activities of the club remained dormant till a move was initiated in 1953, by Sasanka Sekhar Sarkar to form a broad – based organisation accommodating the fifth year students also. The fifth year MSc students who joined and participated were Bikash Roy Choudhury. Arabinda Basu, Pabitra Gupta, Gauranga Chattopadhyay and Biman Das Gupta. The new organisation was named '*Indian Anthropological Society*' and was subsequently registered in 1954 under Society Registration Act, to foster academic discussions, take up publication of journals and monographs, to disseminate Anthropological news and views and the results of researches. The first issue of the journal of Indian AnthropologicalSociety came out in 1966. Dilip Kumar Sen, Surajit Chandra Sinha and Ajit Kumar Danda guided the activities of the journal as Editors at different time periods. Under their stewardship, the journal attained a stature that could accelerate the growth of Anthropology in India.

The year 1921 was also important in another way. In this year Sarat Chandra Roy advocate turned ethnographer, who settled at Ranchi, started the first Anthropological Journal '*Man-in-India*' to document and publish different aspects of Indian culture – tribal, rural and urban. This Journal naturally encouraged Indian scholars and researchers to focus upon the social and economic problems of different strands of population. The journal is still under circulation although its administrative headquarters have now been shifted from Ranchi. Apart from Sarat Chandra Roy, the pioneer Indian ethnographer, eminent anthropologists such as K.P. Chattopadhyay, Nirmal Kumar Bose, Verrier Elwin and Surajit Chandra Sinha were also actively associated with the journal and they worked hard to upkeep its status and glory. After the death of Rebati Mohan Sarkar in 2018, Editor, Man in India, the management of the journal underwent change.[2]

End Note:

1. For the facts noted above I have consulted the Reprint titled'*The Growth of Anthropology in the University of Calcutta'*, by N.K.Syamchaudhury and Shymal Kumar Ray , published in the Bulletin of Anthropological Survey of India, Vol.XXII,1973.
2. The headquarters of Man-in-India was shifted from Ranchi to Calcutta when Dr.Rebati Mohan Sarkar was the Editor. On the death of Dr.Sarkar (death on 18th June,2018), the headquarter of Man in India shifted elsewhere. The journals happens to be the earliest Anthropology Journal in India started by Sarat Chandra Roy from Ranchi.

CHAPTER – II

Some Important Research Studies Made

The teaching of Anthropology on the Post Graduate class missed one thing – there was a dearth of any good book introducing Anthropology. '*An introduction to Anthropology*' authored by D.N. Majumdar and his student T.N. Madan helped the students for decades. This was a book on which students depended for their introduction to Anthropology. In 1970's Gopala Sarana wrote. '*Introducing Anthropology*'. This book was very much useful and handy for students who wanted to know the basis of Anthropology. The next in line was a book titled '*Anthropological Perspectives*' by Biman Kumar Das Gupta, published in 2007. This has been followed by a book written in Bengali titlted '*Samajik Sanskritic Nribigyan*' by Sumohan Bandopadhyay of Vidyasagar University, Medinipur (West Bengal). This book if translated into English could have been helpful for the students. These apart many other scholars have written books introducing the discipline.

In 1920, the Syllabus was finalised by the Board of Higher Studies in Anthropology, Calcutta University. The syllabus also prescribed the different papers that were to be studied for advanced teaching and research in Anthropology.

When the Syllabus was formulated a number of books were recommended for reading in the Post- Graduate classes. Most of the books were authored by Western Scholars. The list, however had the name of a few Indian scholars such as R.P. Chandra (Indo Aryan Races), Bhandarkar (Foreign element in the Hindu Population), Panchanan Mitra (Prehistoric Culture and Races of India) and others. They were the only Indian authors whose books were initially recommended by the University. Gradually Indian scholars who passed out from the Anthropology Department and were involved in research works, published their papers and books and developed and furthered anthropological knowledge in India. Interaction with the western scholars / universities accelerated the pace of Anthropological knowledge in India and Indian scholars developed concepts and tools to study Indian society and culture. Some, however, used endogenous methodology to study Indian culture. Scholars such as Irawati Karve, Nirmal Kumar Bose and Kumar Suresh Singh (who headed the Anthropological Survey of India for number of years, as Director and Director General) developed endogenous methods to undertake national projects. A number of Anthropologists got their PhD's from foreign universities of Asia, Europe and America. Their contact with their foreign guides not only helped to steer Indian Anthropology to a higher level but at the same time popularised the study of Indian Anthropology during the last one hundred years.

During 1960's and 1970's, India saw a book boom. Thematic studies were undertaken by Western Scholars visiting India (such as Oscar Lewis, Morris Opler, A.C. Mayer and others) and also by Indian Scholars in different branches of Anthropology. Say in 1955 three edited books were published in India on village Studies viz, India's villages (ed) by M.N. Srinivas, Indian Village (ed.) by S.C. Dube and Village India (ed.) by Mckim Marriott. These three books have accommodated papers on village study delineated the structure, function, cohesion and conflict in India's villages of different parts of India. In India, villages were units for the study of acculturation, stratification, social movements and for area studies. Village communities were studied and the data analysed to understand the pattern in a Pargana (a conglomeration of villages with a historical, political and cultural tradition). The book *Ethnic Groups, Villages and Towns of Pargana, Barabhum: Report of a Survey* authored by Surajit Sinha, Biman Kumar Das Gupta and Hemendranath Banerjee (published by Anthropological Survey of India, 1966) focused upon regional village communities in evolutionary scale from a stage of uni-ethnic villages to the stage of multi-ethnic, multi-functional villages. Similarly some publications such as '*Agriculture, Crafts and Weekly markets of South Manbhum* authored by Surajit Chandra Sinha, Biman Kumar Das Gupta and Hemendranath Banerjee (published by Anthropological Survey of India, 1961); *Agrarian Situation in India. Vol. I & Vol. II,* edited by S.B. Chakraborty, B.R. Ghosh and Ajit K. Danda (Published by Anthropological Survey of India 1984,

1985); or '*Economic Development and SocialChange in 'South India'* by T.S. Epstein (published by Manchester University Press 1962) can be cited as important and interesting publications on Economic Anthropology in India. Various academic institutes such as Anthropological Surveyof India, the Cultural Research Institutes and Tribal Research Institutes of the states and publication units of different universities of the country and various folklore societies were engaged in publishing monographs on tribal, rural and urban cultures of India during the past few decades. During the middle of the twentieth century a number of Journals of the stature of '*Man-in-India*' (published from Ranchi); *Journal of India Anthropological Society* (that was started by a team of Professors and students of Anthropology of Calcutta University), *Journal of Social Research* published from Department of Anthropology, Ranchi University, first published 1957 and was then edited by L.P. Vidyarthi; *The Eastern Anthropologist* (an organ of Ethnographic and Folk Cultural Society , Lucknow, UP, first published 1947); *The Anthropologist* (Published from Delhi, first published 1970) helped in the dissemination of Anthropological knowledge in the country..

Anthropos India- a mouthpiece of North- Eastern Institute of Cultural Research Guwahati (Assam) and many other journals have helped researchers to disseminate their research findings of scholars. A recent trend, however, is to publish edited books compiling papers on allied topics by authors with expertise on the particular subject (For example, *Tribal Women in India* : 1978; published and edited by Indian Anthropological Society and such other publications). In this context it is necessary to quote the role of Asiatic Society (established 1784) -- [earlier known as Royal Asiatic Society and then named Asiatic Society of Bengal]in providing a platform for Anthropological, historical and linguistic researches in the country.

Dipali Ghosh Danda authored a book on the Dimasa Cachari of Assam ('Among the Dimasa of Assam', New Delhi: Sterling Publisher, 1978) in which she focussed upon the bilineal or double descent system of the Dimasa -- the only of its kind found in India. She delineated beautifully the social and kinship structure. The structural features of the Dimasa, described by her can be placed in the following way. "Each Dimasa boy and each Dimsa girl possesses two sibs –one primary sib and the other secondary sib. For a boy patrisib or father's sib happens to be the primary sib and matrisib or mother's sib happens to be the secondary sib while, for a Dimasa girl, matrisib or mother's sib happens to be the primary sib and patri sib becomes her secondary sib. On marriage a girl sheds her secondary sib (patri sib) and adopts husband's sib as her secondary sib. Patri sib is called *Sengfong* whereas matri sib is called *Jaddi.* A boy is more commonly known by his psatrisib or *Sengfong* whereas a girl is known through her mother's clan. A boy is asked 'what is your *Sengfong* and what is your mother's *Jaddi*? Similarly, a girl is asked what is your *Jaddi* ? What is your father's *Sengfong* ? In the first year, the Dimasa couple follows uxorilocal residences following which the couple will follow virilocal residence'.

'*The Lalung Society: A theme for analytical ethnography*' was authored by N.K. Syam Chaudhuri and M.M.Das. (was Published by Anthropological Survey of India: 1973) accommodates the features of Lalung Society as follows. "The Lalung inhabit the Assam valley and share many tribal traits including the presence of *Chamedi* (bachelors' dormitory) and some non-tribal trait (such as the sacred statue of Mahadev). From their geographical location,it may be accepted that they occupy an intermediate position between the people of two district areas – the Kacharis of the plains and the Khasi tribe of the hills (living in the South and the east of the habitat). Interestingly, the social structural features of the Lalung share features of the patrilineal Kacharis and the matrilineal Khasis."

Among the Lalung of the Assam valley, a number of changes in the social system can be seen. But Shyam Chaudhuri & Das (1973) maintained that inspite of the changes in the residence pattern the matrilineal bias of the Lalung still continued. Quite possible, the Lalung'are showing changes from matriliny to patriliny due to their exposure with the neighbouring patrilineal tribes.

The ethnographic account on the less known tribal group Birija attracted me because of the author's strategy to depict the Birjia Culture in cultural ecological perspective. Samira Dasgupta worked on this small basket making community of Chota Nagpur which is surrounded by larger groups. She identified 'a four step hypothesis to portray the culture of this community which is now identified as PVTG (Particularly Vulnerable Tribal Group) by Ministry of Tribal Affairs, Govt. of India. This book *Birjia; Society and Culture* has been published by M/s Firma KLM Private Ltd. Calcutta in 1994.

Bhabananda Mukherjje worked on a project to analyse the data on social structure, kinship and marriage patterns of the Indian tribes. The data collected by him and other scholars were analysed and interpreted in the backdrop of kinship studies made by western scholars. The salient observations made by him have been noted in his book '*Structure and Kinship in Tribal India'* (published in 1981, by Minerva Associates, (Publications) Private Limited, Kolkata 29.

I was excited to read the study made in the village of 'Sripuram' by Andre Beteille. Although initially the author approached with the idea of understanding a village in the perspective of its relationship with the wider social system but then he explained that his main concern 'has been with the three phenomena of *Caste,Class andPower* (mainly in its political aspects) and with their changing relations'. Beteille focussed upon the interethnic relation between the 'Brahmin, non-Brahmin and Adi-Dravida (untouchables)'. In the book the author described the 'class conflict, shifting of power from traditional to new institutions and the recent changes in the marriage relations. He noted that within the caste system there has been a general trend towards the contraction of structural distance between proximate segments'.

This author also felt impressed to read the ethnographic account of the Meitei of Manipur valley authored by Ranajit Kumar Saha who studied the community as a member of Anthropological Survey of India under the supervision of Nirendra Chandra Choudhury. Saha deserves appreciation because when he started the work staying in the village of Lairenkabi, he did not know the Meitei language. Interestingly, he gradually picked up the language so nicely that he could communicate in Meitei language freely, collected data and prepared a five tier hypothesis to study the Meitei Society culture and their cultural history. In his concluding remarks, Saha noted that the 'Meitei hierarchic, socio-political order around the central institution of kingship arose out of an endogenous structure of clan and lineage based segmentary system'. The results of his field researches have been accommodated in the book entitled "*Valley Society of Manipur*" (Published by Punthi Pustak, Calcutta: 1994).

CHAPTER – III

India Shines: Western Scholars Visiting India

Indian Anthropology has its impact upon the world. L.P. Vidyarthi of Ranchi University was elected the President of International Council of Anthropological and Ethnological Sciences (ICAES), in 1978. Vidyarthi organised the International Congress (as its President) in Vigyan Bhawan, New Delhi, where eminent and rising anthropologists from all parts of the globe met and were exposed to each other. This mega ceremony and academic congregation was inaugurated by the then Prime Minister Shri Morarji Desai.

As a scholar Vidyarthi who had his PhD from Chicago University was known for his study of the *Sacred Complex Gaya*, for his delineation of *Nature- Man- - Spirit Complex among the Maler* and for his study of V*illage Ghagra*.

Nirmal Kumar Bose who later become Director Anthropological Survey of India and then Scheduled Caste Commissioner was an Anthropologist and Human

Geographer of repute published '*Hindu Samajer Garan'* (in Bengali), '*My days with Gandhiji'*, '*Cultural Anthropology'*, '*Canons of Orissan Architecture'* and edited the famous book '*Peasant life in India:a study Indian Unity in Diversity.* Bose's book '*Hindu Samajer Garan'* was later translated into English by Andre Beteille as *'Structure of Hindu Society.'*

II

Western Scholars Visiting India

In the twentieth century, there was a system of appointing foreign visiting fellow in the Anthropological Survey of India. These fellows were mostly eminent scholars (an Anthropologist) and their presence in the host country (India) helped in the exchange of academic dialogue. The Visiting Fellows had their own research projects which they could easily pursue. Side by side they being attached to Head office, Calcutta could deliver talks in other academic institutes of repute such as Indian Statistical Institute, Presidency College and any other Research Centre. Jiro Yonokura, a Human Geographer, came from Japan as Visiting Fellow. He held discussion with the members of the Survey mostly cultural anthropologist and human ecologist. Yonokura took special interest in the study of peasant society through surveying the distribution of material culture traits and constructing the model of India's cultural unity amidst diversity.

Around the middle of the twentieth century a Chinese American Anthropologist FLK Hsu came to India as Visiting Fellow attached to Anthropological Survey of India. The academic interactions that Hsu had with the members of the Anthropological Survey of India were very constructive. It is learnt that Hsu later became the Chairman, Department of Anthropology North Western University. It is interesting to note that. N. Datta Majumdar, Surajit Chandra Sinha, Nirendra Chandra Chaudhuri were PhD's from North Western University and incidentally all these three scholars became Driector or Actg. Director of Anthropological Survey of India later on.

Around 1970, the Austrian Anthropologist C Von F Haimendorf came to Shillong to revisit the Apatani area of Arunachal Pradesh (Apatanis were terrace cultivators, inhabiting Subansiri district of Arunachal). He could undertake his first study among the Apatanis during 1944-45. The Apatani study came as a monograph—'*Apatani and their Neighbours'* and earned reputation for its ethnographic details.Today , the Apatani villages have become very much a part of JFM (Joint Forest Management). JFM has mainly started to check indiscriminate felling of *Texas bacata* (a herb used to cure breast cancer).

CHAPTER – IV

Indian Anthropology and the World

As we learn about the establishment of Post-Graduate course in Anthropology, in India, in 1920, naturally people like to know the status of Anthropological study and research, during 1920's, in the west. In 2020, when Indian Anthropology is one hundred years old, it becomes relevant to assess its march in the perspective of global Anthropology.

Let us recapitulate. Franz Boas the German Cartographer joined the American Arctic expedition and in the end of nineteenth century authored his famous book on the Central Eskimo whereby he asserted the concept of geographical determinism of culture. He contended that the Eskimo culture was by and large the product of Arctic geographical condition in which they lived. Franz Boas later started the Department of Anthropology at Columbia University. Franz Boas is called 'Father of American Anthropology'. In the middle of the twentieth century it was told that all the reputed

American Anthropologists were either the students of Franz Boas or the students' students of Franz Boas. Incidentally, in 1888, another German Scholar Friedrich Ratzel authored a two volume work '*History of Mankind*' depicting tribal cultures exploiting different ecological setting in different parts of the world.

Great Britain was then an important centre of teaching and research in Anthropology and in these respects Oxford University, Cambridge University, London School of Economics and Royal Anthropological Institute were important academic bodies concerned with Anthropology and Sociology. W.H.R. Rivers and his friend A.C.Haddon developed Anthropology Department of Cambridge University with all seriousness. K.P. Chattopadhyay (who later became the Head of Department of Anthropology, Calcutta University) was a student of WHR Rivers had his MSc from Cambridge and returned to India in 1922. From India G.S. Ghurye went to Cambridge in 1922 to work for his PhD under the guidance of W.H.R. Rivers. Due to the untimely death of Rivers, Ghurye had to change his guide and worked, for his PhD, under the guidance of A.C. Haddon. G.S. Ghurye later headed the Department of Sociology, Bombay University, and is known as 'Father of Indian Sociology'.

In the second decade of twentieth century the Polish born British Anthropologist Bronislaw Malinowski worked among the matrilineal Trobriand Islanders for about two years (with some gap between the first and the second trip). He analysed the data proposed the concept of functionalism, discussed with different scholars (especially his mentors) in UK and published his first book '*Argonauts of the Western Pacific*' in 1921. Thus British functionalist school was formally established. (It is known when British functionalist school was formally established, American functionalist R.K, Merton was only eleven years old). During 1920-22, British Anthropology had a galaxy of stars – WHR Rivers, A.C. Haddon, A.R. Radcliffe Brown, Bronislaw Malinowski and then there were K.P. Chattopadhyay, G.S. Ghurye. Only sad thing was that WHR Rivers passed away in 1922. A.R. Radcliffe Brown (who was also a student of WHR Rivers) as Structural functionalist remained a dominant figure in British Anthropology till 1955.

Many of the British colonial officer, (before 1920) devoted themselves to describe the Society and Culture of Indian's population in different parts of this country. In this context it is necessary to mention the monumental works of HH Risley, ET Dalton, PRT Gurdon and others all of whom were responsible for good ethnographic studies. WHR Rivers published the study of the'*Toda*' (of Nilgiri Hills in Tamil Nadu) in 1902; AR Radcliffe Brown's study of the '*Andaman Islanders'* can be cited to be exciting. In 1853,evolutionist Herbert Spencer spoke of struggle for existence and survival of the fittest. In 1859 Charles Darwin (a friend of Herbert Spencer) placed his concept of Origin of Species and Natural Selection. Thus before 1920, Herbert Spencer, Lewis Morgan, EB Tylor and Emile Durkheim already published their famous books in 1882, 1877, 1871, 1893 respectively. Anthropology in India started and developed in a background when Anthropology in the West already had marched forward with themes and models to study society and social dynamics.

II

Since the days Anthropology in India emerged as a discipline Indian Anthropology has been exposed to Anthropology of the west. Western models were used by Indian Anthropologists in studying the Society and Culture and in depicting social transformation and cultural dynamics. A number of Indian scholars visited England, America. Australia and various European countries for higher studies. Scholars from the west (such as Morris Opler, Oscar Lewis. F. G. Bailey and others) visited India for village studies and for studying cohesion and conflict within castes and between castes. But we can name at least three eminent scholars like Irawati Karve (especially her study of kinship system of India); Nirmal Kumar Bose (his material trait Survey of Rural India in connection with his proposed 'pyramid' model to present the type of an unity in diversity in that speaks of the Peasant life in India (published by Anthropological Survey of India: 1961); Kumar Suresh Singh's work on People of India (a proposal conceptualised and completed by him as Director General, Anthropological Survey of India). People of India project very efficiently updated all the earlier ethnographic studies on Indian communities and surveyed the total human surface of the country. The people of India data were compiled in 43 volume (State and Central volume). In these three major studies of India completed by. Mrs. I. Karve, N.K. Bose and Kumar Suresh Singh the methodology adopted was wholly endogenous.

III

During 3rd, 4th and 5th decades of twentieth century, a number of foreign scholars (Anthropologists) visited India to undertake village studies to look into the conflict and cohesion between caste and within caste. Bronislaw Malinowski detailed study of '*Trobraind Islanders*' (near New Guinea) aroused interest in the minds of Sociologists and Anthropologists of the west to undertake community studies. In India too western scholars made it a point to visit and study Indian villages to comprehend their structure, function and quality. The study of 'Rampur village' by Oscar Lewis, 'Madhopur' by Morris Opler,'KishanGarhi' by Mckim Marriott, 'Bishipara' by F.G. Bailey,'Ramkheri' by A.C. Mayer,'Deuli' by GM Carstairs,'Gaon' by Henry Ornestein, 'Namhati' by AR Beals and the Study of Karnataka village by Scarlet Epstein were notable. (Incidentally this was a period when Indian Anthropologists were also seriously involved in village studies e.g., 'Mohana' village studied by DN Majumdar, 'Ghaghra' by LP Vidhyarthi, 'Rampura' by MN Srinivas, 'Shamirpeth' by S.C. Dube, 'Bhangat' and other Barabhum villages by Surajit Chandra Sinha, Biman Kumar Das Gupta and Hemendranath Banerjee, and so on).

Inter-caste relationship, Jajmani system, ritual life, caste hierarchy, conflict and cohesion, rural development and social context in the villages were focussed by the foreign scholars. Such visits by western scholars also facilitated collaborative researches between Indian and Western Universities.

In the second and third decades of 20th century, Edward Jay and Ralph Nicholas (of Chicago University) came to India with two different research projects (on India). Edward Jay worked in the Orcha village of Bastar among a Gond group. His local guide was Surajit Chandra Sinha who was the Head of the Central Regional office, Nagpur, Anthropological Survey of India. Surajit Chandra Sinha had his Ph.D from North Western University and taught in Chicago University for a brief period and was Fellow at Advanced Centre in Behaviorial Sciences, Stanford. Sinha was very much close to Robert Redfield, Milton Singer, Mckim Marriott and others of Chicago University. Ralph Nicholas worked on Caste and Politics in West Bengal. Tarasis Mukherjee, a member of the Anthropological Survey of India was the interpreter of Ralph Nicholas.

CHAPTER – V

Two Foreign Anthropologists and Indian Tribes

Indian Anthropology's delineation remains incomplete without mentioning the contributions of two western scholars, Verrier Elwin and Christopher Haimendorf, both of whom spent a good number of years in India, during 1930-1960's studying tribal culture in the background of India's chequered history.

Harry Verrier Holman Elwin (1902-1964) was educated at Merton College, Oxford. As a student of that college, he showed his proficiency in both theology and English.Very soon on completion of his study,he felt a desire to work under the guidance of Mahatma Gandhi. He came to India as a member of Christ Sava Sangha and settled at Poona. He got interested in India's freedom movement and in 1930, met Mahatma Gandhi and felt elated and inspired to see his life of dedication and his simple life. Gandhiji advised him to work among the tribal people who were economically weak and deprived. Elwin, therefore, chose Bastar that accommodated the Gond and other tribal communities. There he decided to work among the Gond and the Pardhan. Elwin married a Pardhan girl. He became a naturalised citizen of India. He wrote a lot of ethnographic accounts on the Baiga, Muria Gond, Bondo Highlanders and on NEFA (now Arunachal). His book '*Muria and their Ghotul*' brought him a D.Sc. from Oxford University.

Verrier Elwin also held a number of elite government posts. For some years he was a Deputy Director, Anthropological Survey of India and was the Anthropological advisor to Government of Orissa. He worked on the 'Juang' of Orissa. Later, Elwin joined NEFA (now Arunachal) as the Advisor for Tribal affairs to the Governor of Assam (at that time Assam covered a large part of north-east India of course except Manipur and Tripura). Verrier Elwin was considered to be an authority on Tribal areas of north-east India. NEFA was under the administrative control of the Governor of Assam. Elwin was posted at Shillong which was then the headquarters of NEFA. Elwin's knowledge and understanding about tribal problems was also acknowledged by Shri Jawaharlal Nehru- the first Prime Minister of our country. Elwin was quite keen to preserve the tribal culture of the country – their art, music, ethics and values. Elwin wanted that tribal people should not be alienated from their land because that was their greatest economic asset.

Verrier Elwin was an eminent ethnographer. His depiction of tribal customs, tribal cultures, norms and emotions has drawn appreciation from all corners. In the book 'Muria and their '*Ghotul*' (dormitory), he elaborated the '*ghotul*' system that as an institution played pivotal role in the organisation of the society and in imparting training to the youngsters to play a constructive role in the society.Other important publications of Elwin are '*The Baiga'* (1939), '*The Agarias'* (1943),'*Muria murder and Suicide'* (1943),'*Myths of Middle India'* (1947),'*Bondo Highlanders'* (1950), '*Art of NEFA'* (1959), '*Democracy in NEFA'* (1965),'*The Philosophy for NEFA'* (1957), '*The Story of Steel*' (1958) and such other important publication. He died in Shillong (in 1964). His autobiography 'The Tribal world of Verrier Elwin' was published in 1964, albeit posthumously. This autobiographical account of Elwin is excellent and every anthropologist and/or ethnographer will find interest in reading it. The author found this autobiographical account fascinating and was immensely impressed by. Elwin's emotional attachment to the tribal way of life – the music and dances; the art and craft and morals and values of the diverse tribal communities of north-eastern and central India. He felt that tribes should play a significant role in nation building.

In the second decade of twentieth century Christoph Von Furer Haimendorf (1909-1995) joined the University of Venice to study Anthropology and Archaeology. Christoph,in his childhood, was brought up in an elite atmosphere – his father served in the Austrian Civil Service. Christoph himself developed a genuine curiosity to study Indian classic – especially the works of Rabindranath Tagore. Vienna was then under the influence of German diffusionist school or the 'Kultur Kreise School' led by W. Schmidt under whom Christoph also studied. He had his PhD on the 'Tribes of Assam and Northern Burma'. It is learnt that he did not take any field study to prepare his PhD thesis. This probably inspired him later to undertake full field study among a Naga tribe and among the Apatani. Around 1931, he went to London School of Economics to study under the guidance of Polish born British functionalist Bronishlaw Malinowski. He was also interested to establish contact with two other eminent British Anthropologists of those days – Raymond Firth and Andrey Richards. He however, got inspired from the works of Bronishlaw Malinowski. He however, left London to undertake field researches in the hill areas of Assam. In his first encounter in the Naga hills (which was then a part of Assam) he could make friendship with JP Mills. Both went on a trip to an un-administered tribal area between Naga Hills and Burma (now Myanmar). His slim knowledge of Assamese and Nagamese (which he acquired with perseverance) helped him to pursue ethnographic study in that area.

He returned to India to study tribal people in the north-eastern part. This was the period of Second World War, and as he was an Austrian, his presence was not gladly accepted by the British who were fighting against the German. Probably, this was a boon to him. Haimendorf decided to move to Hyderabad which was then under the control of the Nizam. Here he got the opportunity to write two grand ethnographic accounts – one on the 'Chenchu' and the other on the 'Reddi'. He also formulated certain measures to ameliorate the social and economic condition of the Tribal People living in Nizam's territory. However, during 1944-45, Haimendorf was permitted to undertake field studies among the Apatani of Subanseri district (which later became NEFA that was still later named Arunachal).

In 1951, Haimendorf accepted the chair of Asian Anthropology and looked after its Growth and Development. There in the school of Oriental African Studies, he was given some additional academic responsibility. In 1959, he visited the Gond Area of Andhra Pradesh.

Very soon a third area, Napal, was open for him. He received the King Birendra Singh medal from Royal Nepal Academy. He published a number of very interesting ethnographic accounts including the Sherpas of Nepal (1964).

'The Reddis' (1945), 'the Raj Gond of Adilabad' (1948), 'the Konyak Naga' (1963) authored and published by Christoph Haimendorf are memorable works. He had an insatiable urge to study primitive and dynamic culture everywhere. Around 1970, when he visited Shillong to revisit Arunachal, the present author had the opportunity to take him to some craftworkers' villages in Khasi and Jaintia hills. His desire to know the tribal culture meticulously was simply admirable.

Haimendorf's career, as Anthropologist, was spread over forty years. It is learnt that he possessed an excellent collection of photography and video films covering wide range of tribal and primitive culture of the places visited by him. Apart from King Birendra Singh medal , he also won Rivers Memorial prize (1949) and Austrian order of Merit (1982). He possessed unpublished diaries of his visit to different parts of the world documenting his experiences during the active phase of his life.

CHAPTER – VI

Important Researches Done in India: Phases

When we look into different publications and different research projects undertaken by various scholars and institutions in the country, we can identify certain distinct phases. These are:

(a) **Compendium Phase** : When a number of compendia were published documenting ethnographic details of individual communities of region. We can cite the examples of ET Dalton's '*Descriptive Ethnology of Bengal*', Thurston's '*Tribes and Castes of South India*' and so on. These compendia at one time elaborated the culture and the nature of social interaction between groups. These accounts do not provide us with any model to accelerate studies in cultural Anthropology but needless to say these accounts together covered the ethnic surface of the land.

(b) **Individual Ethnographic Phase** :"In this phase a number of valuable ethnographic studies were made on individual tribes describing the distinctive cultural pattern of each. PRT Gurdon's '*The Khasi'*, JH Hutton's '*The Angami Naga'*, W Griffith's '*The Kol'*, TC Das, '*The Purum Kuki of Manipur'* are some examples. We know about the importance of '*ghotul*' (an institution in the life of Maria Gond, from Verrier Elwin's account. We can comprehend the social importance of 'prescriptive alliance system and generalised exchange' from the account left by TC Das. Initially most of these ethnographic accounts were written by British Civilian officials. But we must note that Sarat Chandra Roy was the first Indian ethnographer to write on the Mundas and the Kharia of Chotonagpur in 1912 and 1915 respectively.

(c) **Analytical Phase** : During the fourth and the fifth decades of twentieth century, village studies were taken up by Sociologists and Anthropologists, to portray the structure and function of the village organisation. Village studies also projected the cohesion and conflicts in village life and between castes. '*Caste and Communication in Indian Village'* by DN Majumdar, '*Ghaghra*' by LP Vidyarthi, '*Iravas and their Culture Change'* by A. Aiyappan, '*Santals and their Culture Change'* by N Dutta Majumdar and Village Studies sponsored and edited by MN Srinivas were some of important publications of this phase.

(d) **Conceptualisation Phase**: MN Srinivas' '*Religion and Society among the Coorgs'* spoke of 'Sanskritisation'. LP Vidyarthi's the Maler of Raj Mahal hills' highlighted 'Nature-man- sprit complex concept; Mckim Marriott stressed upon 'parochialisation – universilation'; Surajit Chandra Sinha spoke of 'Tribe- peasant- caste continuum concept. Such conceptual tools furthered anthropological researches in the country and established the method through which empirical data should be collected in India. *At this stage we also come across a number of papers and books, specifically devoted to social mobility movements, authored by DC Sarkar, Mamata Choudhuri, Biman Kumar Das Gupta, KL Sharma, MSA Rao and others.*

(e) **National Survey Phase** : National level surveys can be undertaken only when an institution possesses adequate manpower as well as financial provision to arrange, organise, collect data and complete national surveys within a stipulated period. That is why Anthropological Survey of India could make it possible to propose and complete two mega surveys in our country.

II

Two National Surveys – Two theoretical Premises

Two National Surveys – one during (a) 1959-61 and another (b) during 1985-93 were undertaken and completed by Anthropological Survey of India, the former during the stewardship of Nirmal Kumar Bose, then Director, Anthropological Survey of India and the second during 1985-93 when. Kumar Suresh Singh was the Director General of Anthropological Survey of India.

(a) During 1959-61 an All India Survey on the distribution of Material Culture Traits was undertaken to show the nature of cultural unity in the midst of so called cultural diversity in the country. Data were collected from rural India to locate the differential nature of distribution of 41 material culture traits[1] such as settlement pattern, staple food, dress pattern, oil press, mortar and pestle and so on. In conclusion, NK Bose observed "Village plans in India have certain rough distribution pattern between the northern and the southern part of India. The north is the area of shapeless clusters often breaking up into dispersed unit whereas the southern villages are distinguished by the presence of open streets as integral part of the village layout. Oil press can be distinguished into peninsular type and northern type. In the matter of distribution of material traits a broad regionalism is evident. The form of plough yields to a kind of geographical classification – northern and southern types; but what prevails in the south is extended up to Bihar. The wheels of bullock carts similarly show regional distinction and this becomes clear in the distribution of plough too".

Finally, in his concluding remarks NK Bose remarked "the structure of Indian unity can therefore, be compared to a pyramid. There is more differentiation at the material base of life and progressively less as one mounts higher and higher. It is needless to say that implication is not that the village people are more different from one another than the city people or sophisticated *propertied* class; but that whether it is a villager or a dweller of Indian town, there is more variety in regard to some aspects of life and less in relation to others".

NK Bose's national survey showing the distribution of material trait in rural India and his conceptualisation of the structure of Indian unity were wholly based on indigenous methodology developed by Bose himself.

Before the publication of the book '*Peasant life in India: A study in Indian unity and* Diversity'[2] NK Bose presented his findings (on this National Survey) in a meeting of Anthropologists and Sociologists. There Bose spoke about diversities in culture traits and observed that no specific culture trait could be located all over the land. To this one young (in 1960-61) anthropologist SN Navlakka and another young scholar, cited the examples of 'sacred use of coconut' and the use of '*papad*' (a preparation made from pulses) as two food traits that could be found all over the country. Bose accepted these two examples and assured to check them.

(b) During 1985-93, Kumar Suresh Singh Director General, Anthropological Survey of India launched 'People of India' project to survey the human surface of the country and to update and enrich the ethnographic accounts published earlier. In this project ethnographic account on 4635 communities were collected from 3581 villages and 1011 cities and towns in 421 districts of India.

The methodology followed for the People of India project was very relevant for such a macroscopic project. A blue print of the project was prepared in 1985 by KS Singh himself and the details were discussed with eminent anthropologists of the country. The project schedule was then finalised in a meeting of the senior members of the survey. A complete draft list was made by various regional offices on the basis of the list of schedule caste, scheduled tribes and other communities obtained from Central Ministry of Home and from various census reports and gazetteers. In October 1985, the respective regional offices sent their scientific member on pilot tour, in their respective area so that each member could study one group, prepare a report immediately and present the findings in workshops organised by different regional offices. The first such workshop was organised in Nagpur in November 1985. By December 1985, thus first round of workshops was completed and KS Singh, the architect of the project, attended each session in each region and could immediately prepare plan of work. Members from different regional centres were then sent to different areas, with list already prepared, and collected data on each community and prepared report. The basic data were then transferred to the computer format. Each member submitted abstracts of their reports and the complete reports, all in edited form. This process continued till 1990. The abstracts were accommodated in National volume and the detailed reports in State reports. The computer format helped in preparing scores of tables to facilitate univariate and multivariate analysis of data which again led to understand the qualitative and quantitative profile of the Indian population. Besides the ethnographic volumes the floppies were stored to become a part of the national treasure. This method developed and adopted by KS Singh to complete such a mega project was commendable. The National Informatics Centre, Govt. of India and Centre of Ecological Sciences, Bangalore collaborated with KS Singh at final stage of data analysis.

On the basis of empirical data collected and analysed, KS Singh prepared an Anthropological Atlas (the only of its kind prepared till now). In the preparation of this Atlas (which was finalised by Indian Map Service, Jodhpur), Singh was assisted by the present author and two other senior officers of the Anthropological Survey of India. Oxford University Press printed and published the Atlas in 1993.

End Note :

1. Although data were collected on 41 material traits. The report titled 'Peasant life in India: A Study in Indian Unity and Diversity' was based on 11 traits.
2. N K Bose edited "Peasant life in India: A study in Indian Unity and Diversity" published by Anthropological Survey of India Memoir no. 8; 1961.

CHAPTER – VII

Social Movements

In 1959, Anthropological Survey of India published an account on *Social Mobility Movements among the Tribes and Caste of Central and Eastern India* (Bulletin of Department of Anthropology: Govt. of India, Vol. VIII, 1959). The account covered the social movements of nine communities and the account projected a picture of the range of variations found in these communities (West Bengal – 5, Tripura – 1, Madhya Pradesh – 3). This project was initiated by Nirmal Kumar Bose the then Director of Anthropological Survey of India. While introducing the work, Surajit Chandra Sinha noted ".... the major aim of this book is to be to record the various trends of social mobility movement among the groups described above". Sinha further observed that 'these movements were originally conceived in the context of position in the caste order, have in the past decades been adjusting themselves to various extraneous situation such as the pan-Adivasi movement, General Election, name of the group in the census records, linguistic reorganisation of states etc'.

M.N. Srinivas, conceptual tool of Sanskritisation helped us to study the upward mobility of communities placed in the lower rungs in the regional social order, by emulating clean Sanskritic norms, by avoiding unclean food and occupation. Many communities thus adopted a clean life. This phenomenon could be traced in different parts of northern India.

This kind of upward mobility could not be discerned everywhere, at every corner of the country. There were opposite forces where the lower castes upheld, with dignity, their social status and tried to gain social prestige by all means. We know of *Satya Sadhak Samaj* movement of 1873 started by Jyotirao Govindrao Phule of Maharashtra. He and his wife fought for uplifting education of the children and adults of their community, arranging marriage without the help of Brahman priest and started night schools in their house to promote literacy. We also know of SNDP (*Sri Narayan Guru Dharma Paripalam*) movement of 1903, propagating 'one religion, one god and one caste for all'; SNDP movement worked for the uplift of the Ezhava caste members and other lower castes of Kerala. Temple entry right for all was their demand. In Andhra Pradesh, *Veera Salinjam* established Hitakarini Sabha for the benefit of the poor and poverty stricken people, especially the women. It is known that *Veera Salinjam* rejected superstitions, meaningless ritual and recommended intercaste marriages. In Tamilnadu EVR Naicker worked to establish justice, equality, liberty and fraternity, condemned caste system and rejected Brahmanic domination.Naicker also fought for temple entry right for all the untouchables. EVR Naicker, also known as Thanthai Periyar also started self-respect movement.

Thus it becomes obvious that *Satya Sadhak Samaj* movement, Hitakarini Sabha, SNDP movement and self-respect movement of EVR Naicker walked in a path opposite to 'upward movement' undertaken in some areas of the country.

During 1976-77 when Kumar Suresh Singh was the Director of Anthropological Survey of India, a Seminar was organised by him on the 'Tribal Movements of India' in September 1976. The Seminar was inaugurated by Naga Queen Rani Gaidinliu who not only participated in Mahatma Gandhi's non-co-operation movement but also 'supported the 20 point programme of Prime Minister Indira Gandhi'. The deliberations made in the seminar were accommodated in two volumes – Vol. I exclusively devoted to the tribal movements of north-east India and Vol. II spoke of the movements in other parts of the country. While introducing the seminar, KS Singh noted, 'In the north-east, the tribals are in overwhelming majority; the tribal system (both social and economic) is secure; tribal movements, in this area have essentially been political and secular in nature. In middle India, the situation is far more complex; the tribals have been reduced to minority in many areas and have been exposed to the process of rapid change'. The papers, about fifty in number, delineated the organisation, management and philosophy of such movements and threw light on how these movements had brought transformation in the social system. The leadership factor was also very important along with the role played by press and platform in inspiring people to go for any kind of reform.

In a paper (1978)[1]. Biman Kumar Das Gupta quoted Surajit Chandra Sinha's Rajput myth (1962), and Mamata Chandhuri's (1976) assertion that social mobility had also existed in ancient India. Das Gupta also referred ET Dalton (1872) and HH Risley (1915)'s works to describe that social mobility movements should be understood spatially and historically. Das Gupta placed the tribes of eastern and central India into the following categories –

(1) Tribes living in the plains, in rural areas, maintaining social ties with neighbouring caste groups
(2) Tribes living in the plains, close to the hills, and not much articulated with the neighbouring caste groups.
(3) Tribes living in big and small urban centres being partners of a new social and economic system.
(4) Tribes living in the hills embracing Christianity and maintaining relationship with the regional tribal people
(5) Tribes in the hills in relatively isolated area where they have developed their own system and donot seriously interact with the neighbouring communities
(6) Nomadic and food gathering tribes whose contact with the neighbouring groups is limited and marginal.

Das Gupta described, in brief, the quality of Social Mobility movements seen among the Bhumij, Pahira, Kharia, Santal, Koch, Lalung (West Bengal and Assam), Bhatra, Gond (of Madhya Pradesh), Loi-Chakpa (Manipur). While speaking of the social nobility movements, the author identified four pre-requisites for ongoing social movement such as (a) numerical dominance, (b) settled economy, (c) articulation with neighbouring group, (d) fair literacy rate, (e) good leadership to disseminate message through press and platform.

In fine, three types of social mobility movements can be identified viz;

Integrative : when a group merges its identity with a bigger group

Reformative : When a group revamp its culture without surrendering it identity

Recessive : When the social mobility of a group brings fission within the group

When we discuss about social movements, a few pertinent points emerge.

Any reform movement to alter religions norms and value, will come under social movement. If, however, the movement takes place in the perspective of social hierarchy and is intended to alter the existing status of a group in the regional social hierarchy, the movement should be named Social mobility movement. For example, 'Brahma Samaj Movement' is a Social Movement; but Bhumij –Khsatriya or Rajbansi- Khsatriya movement should be called social mobility movement.

Before 1947, social movements and social mobility movements to improve social status, in the regional social status were relevant in the estimation of different group, occupying low rungs in the social ladder. Instances of movements organised by tribes coming within the Hindu fold, through Sanskritisation or Khsatryisation were plenty. Since 1950 that is since the period adoption of the constitution[2]Scheduled Caste, Scheduled Tribes and other backward classes felt contended with the privileges offered to them through reservation in higher education and jobs. They are happy because through reservation, they expect to achieve a better quality of life. Hence, these communities have been seeing mobility movement with a spirit or redundance and negativity.

Along with social movements, a number of studies have been made in India such as environmental or ecological movement (eg. Chipko movement of Garhwal hill or Appico movement of Karnataka), peasant movement such as indigo revolt of 1859-60 or Tebhaga movement of 1943--1946), women's movement (such as SEWA of Maharashtra or anti-liquor movement in rural Andhra Pradesh). Then there are students' movement, trade union movement and the movement led by various other pressure groups. In all the above cases, it has been seen that movements are planned to bring structural or functional change in the societal system. As a result, the system may temporarily show signs of disequilibrium only to gradually return to a state of social equilibrium.

End Note:

1. 'Social Mobility Movements among the Tribes of Eastern and Central India', in *Journal of Indian Anthropological* Society, Vol. 13, 1978.
2. Constitution was adopted by the Constituent Assembly in November, 1949.

CHAPTER – VIII

Many Ethnographies Studies and One Re-study

In the previous pages we have gone through the wide variety of research projects that were undertaken by various Indian Scholars and a number of foreign anthropologists who worked on Indian tribes, Indian Society and Indian villages. This author was fortunately involved in many of the projects or had to interact with the anthropologists who completed the works with tenacity and lavish sincerity.

Leaving apart the British ethnographers of pre-1947-era, we can mention the works of pioneer Indian ethnographers Sarat Chandra Roy's works on the Mundas(1912) and on the Kharia (1915), DN Majumdar work on the HO, TB Naik's on 'The Bhil', Aiyappan's works on the Iravas; KN Thusu's work on the Dhuwa; N. K. Das study of the Nagas, S. G. Morab's study of the Soliga, William Ekka and AK Danda's account of the Nagasia, Ms. Susheela Devi's work on Paliyan, Ananda Bhanu's work on the Cholanaicken, J.C. Das's study on the pastoral Gujjar and so on. These are just to quote a few to focus upon the diverse, yet united picture of tribal panorama of India.

At this point it has been the feelings of this author that some names of scholars must be noted here to record their lifetime involvement in Anthropological researches. TN Pandit having an encyclopaedic knowledge about the tribal communities of Andaman and Nicobar Islands; Dr. Gouranga Chattopadhya who shifted from mainstream anthropology to management science and held on covetable academic status in IIM Joka (Calcutta); DP Sinha of Ranchi who also shifted to management science; Suhas Kumar Biswas an anthropologist was attached to Indian Statistical Institute and worked on gerontology; the Commendable works of Manish Kumar Raha (who worked in the NW Himalayas) and of Jayanta Kumar Sarkar whose depiction of endangered communities of the Andaman (published in 1993); TS Wilkinson's love for Anthropology and Sociology guided me at Nagpur; KL Sharma's book on Social Stratification; Kamkhenthang's book on the Paite (Manipur), RK Ranjit's work on Manipur Society, Gangumei Kabui's publication on Kabui Naga and such other works, are simply admirable.

This author must admit that he has all through been devoted to two fascinating works viz; '*Modernisation of Indian Tradition*' (1973) by Yogendra Singh and '*Hindu Social Organisation*' (1954) by Pandari Nath Prabhu – these two books have been the guiding force in author's anthropological career.

One Restudy

The Purum Kuki tribal group of South-east of Manipur (Tengroupal district to be specific) had been studied by Tarak Chandra Das of Calcutta University in 1936 but the book was published in 1945 (probably due to the second world war that devastated Eurpoe and Asia during 1939-45). The empirical data on social-cultural norms, economy, village structure, religious beliefs and practices etc. were meticulous and precise. His delineation was thorough and packed with social facts. The task was undertaken by TC Das during the period of the great depression and when Manipur was under the political and social control of the Maharaja of Manipur.

It so happened that 'Purum' population which according to 1931 census was 305, gradually declined alongwith slow rise of a community known as 'Chote' as follows :

1931 Census = Purum 305; Chote 250.
1951 Census = Purum 43; Chote 695.
1961 Census = Purum 82; Chote 1035.
1971 Census = Purum nil; Chote 1905.

This demographic rise and fall attracted the attention of Surajit Chandra Sinha who was a student of TC Das. Sinha was also the Director, Anthropological Survey of India in 1975. Purum Kuki gives us an interesting example of preferential alliance with generalised exchange system. The empirical data documented and presented by T.C. Das attracted the attention of both French Sociologist Levi Strauss (1945) and American Anthropologist Rodney Needham (1950). Levi Strauss felt that matrilateral cross cousin marriage was possible in either matrilineal and patrilineal society 'as long as the system remains harmonic'. Rodney Needham supported Strauss and found in Purum a structure 'analysed and highlighted in a pristine form'. In his famous book 'Structure and Sentiment : a Test Case in Social Anthropology' (Chicago University Press; 1950), Needham described Purum Society drived into (1) one's own descent group, (2) wife giving group and (3) wife receiving group. Among the Purum, 'a clan cannot bring a girl from a clan to which it has given one', thus direct exchange of girl was not possible because that would violate the normative system of marriage.

In fact the Purum type of generalised exchange system with preferential mating pattern and division of the society into three segments, cannot be found in any other tribal group in this area.

Due to this demographic anomaly, the Director, Anthropological Survey of India felt the necessity of restudying the Purum. He sent a team of senior anthropologists (two from cultural anthropology and two from physical anthropology). The team comprised the following members:

Pabitra Gupta, Leader

Biman Kumar Das Gupta (Cultural Anthropologist)

Arabinda Bose (Physical Anthropologist)

Bikash Chandra Raychaudhuri (Cultural Anthropologist)

The team membesr sent by Anthropological Survey of India were asked to take note of the change in population of the community and the type of dispersal of the people, the structural changes in the society, the existing pattern of preferential mating and generalised exchange system etc. The members also took special care to work on the title of the community Purum or Chote. Naturally the team was asked to record the contemporary (during 1975) pattern of economy and cultural dynamics.

But the initial problem was how to start? Incidentally (and luckily for the team), the members could get the album that was prepared by TC Das in the village of *Tampak* where he had started his work in 1936. The album accommodated the photographs with the name, age of the persons who were photographed by Das. The team started from Tampak and found that the Purum were spread over eight other settlements (so including Tampak the number of Purum village were nine). Moreover each Purum village had one contemporary name and one ancient name as follows –

(**Present name**)	(**Ancient name**)	**Population**
Chandropoto	(Fantu)	155
Chumbang	(Faihu)	251
Wangparal	(Purum Khunow)	214
Tampak	(Ahu Faihu)	240
Punthapokpi	(Chotekhunow)	60
Lamlanyhopi	(Lamlangdong)	187
Khongkhang	---	111
Purum Khullen	(Ayoahu)	82
Lairing Khul	(Changliklok)	164

When the team members from Anthropological Survey of India visited the Purum area, nine villages were identified and visited and all of these villages (except the village of Khongkhang) did have some ancient names.

In this context, it strikes to be interesting that in the Purum traditional song only five villages with aliases were mentioned and these were Tampak (Lakhinjaw); Chumbang (Thanhaw); Purum Khullen (Sakherjaw); Lamlanghup

(Chongdom), Khongkhanj (Reinthaw).. TC Das visited four villages:

(1) Purum Khullen with 40 houses
(2) Purum Tampak with 29 houses
(3) Purum Changlinglong with 8/9 houses
(4) Purum Chumbang with 12/13 houses

TC Das also noted that there was 'another village Khongkhang in the eastern part of Manipur bordering Burma'. He also mentioned that a community called 'Chote' lived in a village called Lamlanghupi near Bishenpur.

However, on returning from the field, the data were placed (in the form of paper) in a symposium organised in 1983 in Calcutta. The symposium was attended by twenty two scholars of the Survey, from different institutes, and of Universities including two educated Purum (Chote) members. The proceedings of the Seminar were published[1] in 1985. It was decided to refer the group as Purum (Chote) "because the people refer them as Chote but others call them as Purum."

Thus, it was clear that we were in the midst of Purum villages during our field stay in 1975,some had 'ancient' name with aliases whereas some village names were recorded in the traditional songs and there were certain other villages that were not recorded in TC Das' book. At the same time , the ethnic names 'Purum', Chote' and Purum (Chote) were in use. Some village like Khanghang was in the eastern most part, some were centrally located, and some such as Lamlanghupi was considered to be the western most village. The Purum population of 303 (of 1936) was in 1975 found to be 1464, Thus the nine Purum (Chote) villages may be clubbed as central group (7 villages), eastern most

Khongkhang and the western most Lamlanghupi. These Purum (Chote) categorise the neighbouring population as – *hao* (other hill people), Wanchu (Meitei) and *abing* (outsider). The dialect of the Chote called '*Choterim*' was distinguished from *haorin* (dialect of other hill people).

Among the Purum (Chote), the village council was divided into *hloukal* (guild of elders) and *Loumi* (guild of youngsters); male household deity is *Sanamahi* and the female household deity is *Laimren*; marrying cross cousin (MBD) was considered superior type of marriage *achumpihak* and other type of marriage was *pihak*; bride giving group was considered superior and '*amphing*' and the bride receiving group inferior i.e. *alakpheng*. Every village had a village council. In the eastern most village of Khongkhang the village council was called *fomnei*. In the non-christian village of Lamlanghupi (Western most village) *Pipa* or the lineage chief was found to possess important role in prescribing andmanaging rituals.

The revisit in the villages of Purum (Chote) i.e. a restudy of the Purum (Chote) data vis-a-vis T.C. Das path breaking ethnographic document of the Purum helped us to locate a number of important aspects that slowly changed the structure and functional aspect of Purum (Chote) social-cultural institutions. These are noted below :

Traditionally, the Purum (Chote) had five sibs and including sub sibs the number was said to be ten. But often they told of having seven sibs and hence they cited that their village council accommodated seven member belonged to seven sibs. But during our restudy it was seen that Purum (Chote) belonging to nine villages were affiliated to twenty-seven sibs and sub-sibs. Moreover, no village was found where all the twenty-seven sibs could be located. The two sibs, *Hiyang* and *Pirring* were actually sibs conferred upon Kabui Naga men when they married Purum (Chote) girls.

As per generalised exchange system with prescriptive alliance, a sib could give bride to a particular sib but could receive bride only from prescribed sib or sibs. It meant that direct exchange of bride, between sibs, was not allowed. But during the revisit, out of 255 marriage cases (collected through village level census) direct exchange of bride between two sub sibs, was recorded in twenty one cases.

In view of their contact with the various tribal groups around them and since marriageable partners were not always easily available, in fortyone cases marriages between Purum (Chote) and non-Purum (Chote) boy and girls were recorded. These non-Purum (Chote) boys and girls were from Anal, Kabui, Tangkhul, Hmar, Mao and Moyon groups.

In the paper written in the symposium proceeding volume, Biman Kumar Das Gupta noted that 'Symbolic order is a stable order and symbolism as an integral part of culture cannot undergo any change'. In fact, a social structure and alliance pattern similar to those found among the Purum cannot be found in any other group in north east India. Moreover, such a symposium in which two educated persons of the group participated and took part in the deliberation can rarely be found. The two educated Purum (Chote) persons took special interest in our field researches and while empirical data were collected, both Mr. Abersing Kankung and Mr. Maipak Yuhllung were fascinated and extended helping hand to the team.

Through the restudy the following important points could be highlighted –

- In the eight villages (of central and eastern cluster) the role of '*pipa*' was fully eclipsed.
- The revisit could help us to locate that except Lamlaughupi (eastern most) village the people of all the other eight villages were converted into Christianity. Therefore, many traditional institutions became dysfunctional.
- The revisit helped us to speak that Chote General Union as a body to bind the people into one political body had started since 1946. Between 1946 to 1975 nine meetings were organised by the CGU. The CGU was first started in the village of Tampak and incidentally our restudy started from this village too. In the meantime the youths of the Purum (Chote) group formed Chote Naga StudentsUunion (CGNU) which became affiliated to Naga students union and not to AMSU (All Manipur Student union). From 1972 the CGNU became affiliated to Naga student federation (NSF). In this context, it can be noted that Manipur North District Naga Students Association was also affiliated to NSF.
- In short, the revisit reflected that the Purum (Chote) were not found to be a dwindling population; They existed adopting the ethnic name Chote and they were spread over nine villages.
- Due to population explosion, there was a tendency to go for settled cultivation in the valley by moving to newer sites for bumper production of cereal crops. Side by side, with cereal crops, the Purum

(Chote) started producing cash crops to become *achongpa* (rich). As a mark of their better economic status, it was seen that many of Purum (Chote) peasants possessed *inlok* (big house) abandoning the practice of staying in *inte* (small house).

- The eastern most village of Khongkhang was still located in the hill slopes. But other bigger villages (such as Lairingkhul, Tampak, Chondropoto) shifted to valley cultivation, due to denudation of forests. However, side by side with agriculture, they also produced cash crops such as banana, chilli, potato and millets in the *pamlou* plots where swidden cultivation was still practised. The change in the location of villages gave them better access to valley economy and valley market. The emergence of cash economy resulted in the rise of two distinct classes *achongpa* and *saropa* (i.e. rich- poor).
- Every village was found to be equipped with a *hupal* (village council) with seven officials – *hulak, huklak, hunchal, yupal, keirung, selrung* and *changrui*. The village elders selected this body. The village head *hupal* had to deal with all important village matters. In fact the *yupal* was found to comprise *hloukal* (elders' body) and *loumi* (youngsters' body). The *loumi* was also found to possess all the seven officials. Any dispute was independently adjudicated by the two bodies and in case the two bodies differed in their adjudication the matter was referred to a *tarpu*-- oldest member of the village.
- So far as the posts of village chief were concerned in the villages of Khongkang (easternmost) and

Lamlanghup (westernmost), the post was found to be hereditary, whereas in the villages of central cluster the villages, chief was elected. Therefore, the Purum (Chote) of these two village argued that they were the original 'chote'. In the village of Khongkhang, the village chief was found to perform the important task of allocating *Pamlau* plots. In Lamlanghup, the role of *pipa*, as lineage chief, was quite conspicuous.

It is therefore seen that the re-study could locate the following points--

(1) population rise and population dispersal to nine village (from original 3-4)
(2) total conversion of the population to Christianity in eight villages (during 1936-75) and turning many traditional institutions dysfunctional, attenuated or eclipsed.
(3) avoiding swidden cultivation in favour of wet cultivation along with the movement of the settlement towards the valley to be closer to valley market and valley economy
(4) emergence of cash economy and production of cash crops leading to the appearances of economic classes and
(5) political parties and political affiliation gradually embracing the Purum Chote can be noted to be some salient findings of the re-study.

End note:

1. Proceedings of the Symposium Purum (Chote) Revisited edited by. Biman Kumar Das Gupta et al, Calcutta: Anthropological Survey of India, 1985.

CHAPTER – IX

Author's involvement in Anthropological Projects

My first field research (as a member of Anthropological Survey of India) was in the now defunct Pargana of Barabhum (which was a part of erstwhile Manbhum) – Barabhum was a multi- ethnic tribal estate in the Western part of the West Bengal. The Rajah (a tribal chief) was a Bhumij but he under the influence of Hinduism appointed Brahman priests to preside over rituals in the palace temples; he donated villages to the Brahman priests to perform important rituals especially the *Ind parab* (propitiation of God Indra) in the month of September. In this ceremony, two umbrellas were raised, first in the name of the Indra and the second in the name of the king signifying that the king received the blessings of the God *Indra*. This ceremony was attended by thousands of people (of Barabhum) who accepted it as divine blessings for their kings. This ritual helped the king to keep his subjects under control. This ritual was graced by all the tribal leaders of the Parganna especially they who accepted the king as their leader. This major ceremony was followed by a month long fair which was attended by various traders (petty) of the area. This Pargana comprised 596 villages, inhabited by tribes and non-tribal people. The villages varied from uni-ethnic, bi-ethnic to multi-ethnic ones. There was also a small town Balarampur that developed through orthogenetic process as the settlement was an important lac growing and lac trading centre. However, the fair that was held at Barabazar (Barabhum Rajah's headquarters) grew into stable economic institution. The Hinduisation of the king and his agnates paved the way of stratification of Bhumij Society into *ataisey, nagadi* and *nichu.*

The Barabhum estate (Pargana) had a hierarchie feudal structure. The king was the owner of all the 596 villages. The king allotted 100 or more number of villages to his four / five *Sadiyals*. Below the *Sadiyals* were a number of *Taraf Sardars* each owner of 50 to 60 villages; below the *Taraf Sardars* were a number of *Ghatwal* each heading 1 to 4 number of villages. Thus the feudal hierarchy ran in the following pattern :

Raja

↓

Sadiyal

↓

Taraf Sardar

↓

Ghatwal

It was mandatory for the *Sadiyals*, *Taraf Sardars* and *Ghatwals* to pay a visit to the king with locally available products as gift. Some of these leaders in the feudal hierarchy also celebrated *Chata parab* (in the way *Ind Parab* was celebrated in the King's headquarter). The *Taraf Sardar* of Gobarghusi also organized *Chata parab* (that was attended by the present author with his team) with reasonable pomp and éclat. The present author made an overnight trip to Gobarghusi (from Barabazar, King's headquarter). The *Taraf Sardar* was glad to find the author and his team, in his house and in the ceremonial ground entertained us with tea and snacks. We returned from Gobarghusi a little before evening and the *Taraf Sardar* sent a group of young men with spears etc. to escort us till the end of his *Taraf* boundary. (It was a midnight of 1958).

This research project (As a part of Area Study Barabhum sponsored by Anthropological Survey of India) was taken up to establish "what happens when a tribal estate disintegrates and how a new set of political control replaces a traditional political order".

In Shillong the present author was posted from 1960 to 1973 and was involved in various assignments. This period was very colourful and the author was overwhelmed with joy to work in the cultural mosaic of North- East India. Initially, the task was to chalk out a picture of pattern of territorial distribution of traditional crafts in Khasi and Jaintia and Garo hills (which later, formed into Meghalaya). In the PnarKhasi area there were potters; in the Bhoi Khasi area (close to the Assam valley) the Bhoi Khasi were involved in art of silk worm rearing and silk weaving; the War Khasi area basket making happened to be the major economy in the rural area due to the abundance of bamboo groves; in the central part of Khasi hills again one could find blacksmith as a primary occupation for many. In this area once the village of Laitdom flourished as an ancient centre where iron smelting was done in primitive way.

In the next couple of years, as a part of All India Survey of Pottery Techniques and Potters, the north- eastern part of the country was also covered. In Assam, in fact, two types of potter groups were found – the Kolita who produced wheel made pottery and the Hira who made handmade pots. The pots made by the Hira were used for ritual purpose also.

1964 was a productive year for the author. As a member of a research team (team was led by R.S.Negi) of Anthropological Survey of India, the 'Tribal Stratum of Sikkim's Population' was covered. Sikkim was then an independent Kingdom. We met the then Maharaja of Sikkim--His Highness Namgyal, the Indian Political Officer- Avtar Singh and the Diwan of the Maharaja--R.N. Haldipur. The northern part happens to be an area of the Bhot (who are Buddhist, pastoral and practised transhumance).The central Zangu Valley is inhabited by the Lepcha and the western part is populated by the Napalese. In the north the author with the team camped at Lachen and Lachun to study the Bhot society and culture and to document the monastery system and monastery network. The author first camped in the beautiful and picturesque Synghik (which was then within Mangan district) and the thrust was to understand the cultural centres of their Himalayan Kingdom and to identify the forces that kept the different ethnic group together. The details of Pemyangtse monastery, the Lachen monastery and the Rungpo monastery gave a very interesting picture of the ecclesiastical system of Sikkim which, in those days, was a theocratic state. Buddhism was state religion of Sikkim. Side by side, the impact if transhumance, polyandry were also noted. Sikkim was then a vibrant tourist spot too.

During 1965-67 there was a demand to unknot the phenomena of Koch – Koch Khsatnya – Rajbansi and Rajbansi-Khastriya phenomenon. The study was undertaken in Goalpara district (Assam) and Jalpaipuri – Coochbehar districts (West Bengal). Side by side with the study of social system of the communities care was taken to comprehend the details of social mobility movement among the community where various efforts were undertaken since 1911, to elevate the social status especially following the path of reforms charted by Thakur Shri Panchanan Roy Burman- the great social reformer. The present author spent his school days in northern part of West Bengal where he interacted and articulated with Rajbansi boys. One such senior friend of his was Shri Amar Roy Pradhan who later became MP (for eight terms between 1977-99). In the young days the author found. Amar Roy Pradhan as a political figure who worked for the welfare of the needy and disseminated the ideology of Thakur Panchanan too. The establishment of North Bengal University helped the Rajbansi boys and girls to receive higher education easily. The elite educated class among the Rajbansi led the desire to enrich Kamatapuri language and work for its better academic status.

Later, however, the *Rajbansi Khsatriya Samity* activities concentrated more centering Siliguri which gradually became a cosmopolitan urban centre. Siliguri happens to be the gateway of Sikkim, Nepal, Bhutan and Assam. Moreover Siliguri gradually became influenced GNLF and later by the activities of GJM. The *Rajbansi Khsatriya Samity* members also felt that their demand would get more publicity in Siliguri because of its cosmopolitan character. Therefore, the head office of *Rajbansi Khsatriya Samity* (which was originally located at Rungpur in Bangladesh) shifted from Jalpaiguri to Siliguri. The proximity to the North Bengal University was also factor for this shift.

During 1968-69 this author visited Arunachal Pradesh and studied the Gallong, the Minyong and some communities of the Adi group. The author entered (with two colleagues) through Silapathar (by train) and then by bus and camped at Along, Pangin, Kabu ,Pasighat and some other neighbouring villages and settlements. Both these tribal groups were shifting cultivators. The Minyong were horticulturist too growing oranges in plenty. But due to difficulties in transportation, these oranges, at that time, could not be sold either in the Along market or in the Pasighat market. Though we entered through Silapathar, we returned via Pasighat crossing the Brahmaputra in a motorised boat.

In the Gallong Minyong area, the thrust was to document the system of polyandry, bachelors' dormitory (*deyere*) and village endogamy among the Gallong. The structure and function of the girls dormitory (Ri sheng), moiety organization and the alliance norm among the Minyong were studied. It was our desire to get into the social structure, the traditional social system and the ritual laden life of these tribal groups. (Lower Siang People – P. Lal and Biman Kumar Das Gupta, Calcutta: Anthropological Survey of India, 1979).

Study was also focused on how these two tribal groups with different types of social system and social structure could maintain social equilibrium in the midst of immigrant non-tribal population in the district headquarter- Along and the trading centre Pasighat. Effort was also made to identify why some traditional institution and cultural traits gradually were becoming dysfunctional and what was its impact.

The year 1969 took the team to spectacular cultural stratum in Manipur – that was in connection with the Area Study Manipur project work. Manipur is a picturesque state of our country where the centrally located Imphal Valley is densely populated. Here the Meitei are pursuing Gauriya faith whereas some are affiliated to traditional Sanamahi faith. The Meitei literature grew using Bangali Script. During 1969-75, when the author was involved in a cross- cultural study in the valley ,a section of the literati class expressed their desire to shift to the script which they had used earlier (i.e. before they used Bengali Script).

The ethnic structure of Manipur appeared to the author as simply unique. The central valley inhabited by the Meitei; the northern part by Zemi-Langmer-Rongmei Nagas; the southern part by the Kuki groups such as Paite, Veiphei, Purum. In the southern part again, around the Logtak Lake in the marshy area, we found the Yathibi; in the eastern border between the hills and the plains (i.e. where the hills and the plains meet) we found Loi Chakpa population especially in the big Loi Chakpa villages of Sekmai, Phayeng, Andro and others. *Leiharoba*- the spring festival, was found to be celebrated in the big villages of the valley with pomp and éclat. The tribal people, many of them became Christians, celebrated their festival as per schedule. Amidst diversities certain ceremonies were organized in and around the palace where different strands of population congregated. In the valley, near the Palace of the Maharaja of Manipur a few congregations were organized by the Maharaja. One such occasion was *hiruhitongba* or boat race in which the tribal Chiefs had an important role to play. The boats, used in this race, were made in the Kabui Naga villages. The other occasion was *haochongba* i.e., tribal performance in which the tribal groups from different parts of the state gathered and performed tribal dances.

These festivals held close to the Palace, made them aware of the superarching power of the crown – a supremacy that was accepted by all when Maharaja's political power was active. In such gathering every tribal group attended in their traditional attires with scarfs.

The ethnic diversity among the tribal people of Manipur in the hills of the northern, southern, eastern parts shared some common elements viz. swidden cultivation, allegiance to animism or Christianity, presence of bachelors' dormitory (among the non-christian), small bi-clan or tri-clan settlements, typical attire for each group and a general consciousness of belonging to a particular group. On the contrary the valley Meitei were found to worship household deities *Sanamahi, Laimren*, celebrating *Leiharaoba* festival, propitiating *Umonglei* (forest god), applying sandal wood paste on the forehead (especially by those who followed *Gauriya* faith), upholding the ritual authority of lineage chief-*pipa*; affiliation to any of five yeks and accepting the relationship between territory and yek.

In the context of Area Study : Manipur the distribution of salient traits was also studied cross-culturally. The picture placed below:

	Valley Meitei	**Loi-Chakpa**	**Plains tribes**	**Hill tribes**
Loisang (Sacred deity)	At palace	At village	Absent	Absent
Settlement type	Big	Big	Small	Small
Umonglei (forest god)	Present	Present	Absent	Absent
Laimren Sanamahi (hosehold deity)	Present	Present	Present	Absent
Funga (Sacred fire)	Present	Present	Present	Absent
Worship of Lord Krishna	Present	Present with a school	Absent	Absent
Christianity	Not found	Not found	Among some present	Present among some
Occupational specialization	Agricultur, Weaving, Fishing, Smithy. …	Settled agriculture, pot making, silkworm rearing	Settled agriculture, swidden cultivation	Swidden Cultivation

In Manipur, indigenous classification of land was followed in terms of use, fertility of soil and price structure etc.

(1) Pamlau

(2) Inkhon

(3) Fawren

(4) Anganphow

(5) Taukthabi

1 = hill top land used for swidden cultivation
2 = residential area: (cost less than *anganphow*)
3 = fawren is the best type cultivatable land which give maximum crop and good quality paddy: (costliest land)
4 = in the matter of crop yield and quality of paddy, *anganphow* is only second to *fawren.* (in cost, next to fawren..)
5 = mainly marshy land and located around Logtak lake. Minimum crop yield (Least costly)

We found a close relationship between ethnic group and gradation of land. For example *taukthipi* land was found to be inhabited by the Yathibi with low social status; the two better types of arable land were in the hand of Meitei and Loi-Chakpa.

From 1983-88, as a senior Anthropologist the author was attached to the Central Regional Office, Nagpur, where for some years he had to perform administrative jobs steering anthropological research projects in this Regional Office;

It was the period when under the guidance of Director General K.S. Singh he got the opportunity to monitor the People of India Project activities in Maharashtra, Madhya Pradesh and Goa. It was a great experience and details are already elaborated in some previous paragraphs under 'National Project'. It was a time bound project that took into account the task of depicting the cultural interaction between different communities of the country. The strategy of computerizing the colossal ethnographic materials and the projection of the data with a national perspective was a genuinely pioneer effort made by the Director General (K.S. Singh). This experience has been exciting for me.

CHAPTER – X

Indian Tribes

Today, tribes in Indian comprise 8.6% of the total population of the country. Punjab, Haryana, Delhi, Chandigarh and Pondichery (Poduchary) do not have any tribal component in their population. According to 2001 census, Goa has only 0.04% tribal population. States with high percentage of tribal population are Mizoram (94.46), Nagaland (89.15), Meghalaya (85.34) and Lakshadeep (94.57). The states such as Jharkhand, Chhattisgarh and Uttaranchal that have been curved out from Bihar, Madhya Pradesh and Uttar Pradesh respectively, in 2000, do not have a high percentage of tribal components. When India achieved freedom, the percentage of literacy among the tribes was only 7 percent. This percentage improved to 8.5 in 1961, to 11.29 in 1971 to 16.35 in 1981, to 24.32 in 1991, to 47.10 in 2001 and to 69.4 in 2011.

Magnificent improvement in the field of literacy and education has been mainly due to missionary zeal of the people as well as of the government and the constitutional provisions that are already there. The government has today envisaged a uniform educational programme for the tribal people so that they can know the regional culture as well as the national culture. Medium of instruction, appointment of educated local teachers, opening of '*asrama*' type of school, provision of free supply of books and subsidized hostel accommodation are some of the measures taken by the government.

The tribal canvas of India is simply varied. There are small tribal communities such as Onge (Little Amdaman) or Shompen (The Nicobars) and there are large tribal communities such as Gond, Munda, Santal, Ho, Oraon (of central India) and Bhil (western India). Santal, Munda, Ho, Bhil are patrilineal whereas Khasi and Garo (Meghalaya) are matrilineal and Dimasa (Assam) are bilineal. The patrilineal groups follow patrilocal or virilocal residence and matrilineal groups follow matrilineal or uxorilocal residence (In patrilocal residence after marriage the wife comes to live in the husband's house whereas in matrilocal residence after marriage the husband comes to stay in the house of that wife). The matrilineal Pnar Khasi (Meghalaya) follow duolocal residence. The Dimasa of Assam, however, practise '*minhaba*' – after marriage the newly wed boy and girl stay in the wife's house but after that they go to the husband's house to spend the rest part of their life. Bhumij, Munda, Santal, Ho are agriculturists. Juang (Orissa), Koya (Andhra Pradesh) Gallong (Arunachal) are shifting hill cultivators. Birhors (West Bengal, Jharkhand) and Mankids (Odisha) are nomads. Andamanese, Jarawas are hunters and gathers;

Todas (Nilgiri Hills – Tamil Nadu) and Bhotia of Sikkim are pastoral people. Kolis (Maharashtra) are also fishermen who are marine fisherfolk too. Nagas (Nagaland), Apatani (Arunachal) practise terrace cultivation. The Rabari of Gujrat also cattle herders. Rabaris and Todas are vegetarians but the Todas take ritually sacrificed buffalo's meat once a year. Most of tribal communities are monogamous but Toda, Bhotia, Gallong practise polyandry. Khasas are polygynandrous. The Purum Kuki marry following the norms of generalised exchange and prescriptive alliance system (direct exchange of girls between clans is not allowed among the Purum). Gonds and Lalungs have phratry system and about 30 tribal groups have moieties; Minyongs (Arunachal) have very interesting moiety system that regulate their marriages.

There are 166 tribal speeches in the country. Many of the tribes use Roman scripts as the Khasi, Mizo or the Munda do. The Santal have developed their own *Ol-chiki* script with the belief that the script may be fruitfully used for other languages under Austric family. Many of the central Indian tribes (except the Oraon), the Nicobarese (Nicobar islands), Khasi (Meghalaya) belong to the Austric family. Most of the tribes of north-east India (except the Khasi) belong to the Tibeto – Burman language family. In South Indian the Toda do not speak any language belonging to Dravdian family. All Austric speaking groups are tribes but all tribes are not Austric Speakers.

Broadly speaking, the tribes of India can be grouped into the following zones.

North East Zone : Arunachal tribes such as Monpa, Aka, Sherdukpen,Apatani, Dafla, Gallong, Minyongs, Boru, Boker, Pasi, Khamti, Mishmi, Tangsa, Nocte.

Naga group such as Ao, Sema, Angami, Rengma., Tangkhul, Zemi, Lang Mei, Kabui.

Mech, Lalung, Rabha, Dimasa of Assam;

Khasi, Garo of Meghalaya;

Purum, Anal, Paite, Chote of Manipur;

Simte, Lushai, Poi, Lakher of Mizoram;

Lepcha, Bhotia and Nepali speaking group of Sikkim.

East Zone : West Bengal tribes such as Santal, Bhumij,Mahali, Kora Mudi;

Jharkhand tribes such as Munda, Ho, Maler, Binjhia;

Orissa tribes such as Juang, Khond,Bhuiya and other.

Central Zone : Comprising Gond group of Madhya Pradesh: Baiga, Kamar, Pardhan of Madhya Pradesh;

Pando, Korwa and others of Chhattisgarh;

Bhil, Katkari Thakur, Koli of Maharashtra.

North- West : Tharu of Uttar Pradesh; Lahuli and Spitial of Ladakh.

Western Zone : Siddi, Varli, Rabari of Gujarat; Bhil, Mina of Rajasthan; Beda, Balti, Chengpa, Mon of Jammu and Kashmir.

South Zone : Malaulldan, Toda of Tamil Nadu;

Sholiga,Korava of Karnataka.

Kurumba, Cholaraicken of Kerala.

Chenchu, Koya and others of Andhra Pradesh.

Island Zones :

Eastern Island :	Covering Andamanese, Jarawa, Onge of Andaman islands; Car Nicobarese and Shompen of Nicobar group of islands.
Western Island groups :	Accommodating groups such as Thakru, Thakrufan, Koya, Malami, Melechari, Raveri of Lakshadeep.

In this vast yet very colourful tribal canvas of this country, a few interesting features can be noted. These are –

a. Nordic tribe living in the Dravidian milieu of the south
b. Dravidian speaking Oraons living in the Proto Austraoid milieu
c. Austric speaking Khasis are found in Tibeto-Mongoloid milieu of NE
d. Indo Aryan speaking Nahal-korku in the Dravidian area
e. Austric speaking Nicobarese living in the Eastern Island Zone.

CHAPTER – XI

Indian enjoys Ethnic diversity of the land

"Let us unite, not inspite of our difference
But through them –
For differences can never be copied away
and life would be poorer without them"

– Rabindranath Tagore : Talk in China

The population of India has always been heterogeneous. History records how different ethnic groups from different parts of the world visited the exquisite land for trade for exchange of ideas and to the royal courts at different periods. Sakas, Huno, Pathans and Mughal came from Asia, Siddi (found in Gujarat) came from Africa, the British, French and the Dutch came from Europe. Some came through land routes whereas others came by sea. European and other traders came in search of spices, cotton and metals. In fact, sea routes were discovered for the purpose of trade between continents. Initially contact between people was transient but gradually migration of people from outside India became a phenomenon and has left far reaching impact. Migration of people into India resulted in inter-ethnic relationship and intermarriages. This led to emergence of newer and newer types of people. N.K. Bose et al in this write, "when members of one physical type migrate to the place of another, the two remain roughly distinguishable over a long period of time unless there is free intermarriage. This is of importance in history. The civilization of a country is built up by various communities and if the facts about the origin and migration of those communities are reliably established through the study of biological characteristics, the study of the history of civilization will be helped as well." [N.K. Bose, A. Mitra, P Gupta and Harshanath Mukherjee, "The People," published in Gazettes of India, Indian Union : Vol. I. (Country and People) 1965].

This kind of migration and movement of people from one country to another have two effects.One, it helps in contact of people resulting in exchange and flow of cultural traits and helps in globalization of culture. Secondly, the maritime trade helped in making certain countries naval powers. Hence we find that the Asian traders were naval powers and could establish colonies in different countries of Asia and Africa. Traders became rulers. India's resources were utilised by the colonial rulers but then India also got a test of industrialization. British rulers in India accelerated the spread English education and at the same time patronised the desire of a class of people to bring social reforms and to do away with prejudices.

India today accommodates about 4635 communities (vide people of India project sponsored by Anthropological Survey of India) belonging to nine religious groups (bends the tribal belief systems of 427 tribal groups) that pursue about 376 main/or subsidiary occupations and speaking 496 languages including 166 tribal dialetes. British rulers classified Indian population into three social categories – Hindus, Muslims and tribes. Independent India has restructured the classification into scheduled caste, scheduled tribes, Denotified tribes, other backward communities, minority communities and population under general category. This has been done to suit the social and political aspiration of different communities and of various states of India.

At least four Anthropologists/administrators have attempted to classify Indian communities. The first was C.Von Eickstedt who studied India's population (from biological point of view) during 1920-23 and classified India's population into Indid, Veddid, Malid (comprising North Melanid and South Melanid), Nordid, Dinarid, Alpin, Mediteranean, Palaeo-Mongoloid; Orientalid. According to Eickstedt (whose original classification came out in German language), the Dinarid and Alpin elements were mainly responsible for brachycephalisn in India.

In this context, it would by pertinent to put that before Eickstedt, two other scholars made attempts to classify the population of India through somatometry and somatoscopy. One was Charles de Ujfalvy in 1881-82 who measured a number of individuals in western Himalayas and Hindukush. This was followed by the endeavour by captain Drake Brockman who in 1886 took measurements (somatometric) of about four thousand individuals in Uttar Pradesh. The measurements and Brockman's observations were quoted in the book 'Tribes and Caste of North Western Provinces' authored by W Crooke (Bose et al : 1963).

Herbert Risley's classification of the first decade of twentieth century is important because he used certain terms different from those mentioned by Eickstedt. In Risley's views the racial types found in India are - Turko Iranian; Indo Aryan, Scytho Dravidian, Dravidian, Aryo Dravidian, Mongolo Dravidian, Mongoloid and Negrito of Andamans. Risley has observed that the Mongoloids were mainly responsible for brachycephalism in the eastern part of India whereas the Seythian element infused brachycephalism in the western part. Risley's contention that brachycephaljian in India is largely due to Monogoloid influence, has been criticized by noted Indologist R.R Chanda.

In 1931 Biraja Sankar Guha (who later became the founder Director of Anthropological Survey of India) prepared a comprehensive report. Today Guha's observations stand as the first racial classification (of India's population) by any professionally trained anthropologist. Guha has proposed the following classification - Negrito, Proto Australoid, Mongoloid comprising Palaeo Mongoloid and Tibeto Mongoloid, Mediterranean consisting of Palaeo Medeterranean, Mediteranean and Orientals, Western Brachycephals comprising Alpine, Dinaric and Armenoids and Nordic. Guha has also detailed the major somatometric and somatoscopic characters of the racial elements. These are Negrito with woolly/frizzly hair, pygmy stature, dark complexion, bulbous forehead, steatopygia among women and thick lips. Proto Australoids with wavy hair, platyrrhine nose, broad bizygomatic arch, dark complexion, thick inverted lips and medium stature. Mongoloids have been described as having epicanthic fold, broad bizygomatic arch yellowish skin colour, scanty hair on face and body and straight hair on the head. Of the Mongoloid, the Tibeto mongoloid subgroup is tall whereas the Palaeo mongoloid have medium stature. Among the Mediterraneans Guha has identified three types (a) Palaeo Mediterranean or Proto Egyptian identified from ancient skeletal remains (b) Main Mediterranian who were primarily responsible for the Indus Valley civilization and the (c) third type termed as the Oriental or eastern type. The tall fair large faced western brachycephals with high cranial vault have three types - Alpine, Dinaric, Armenoid. In fact Guha has suggested that brachyceplisim in India has come from the Western brachycephals. Guha has described the Nordics as sturdily built, tall having dolicho or brachycephalism, leptorrhiny and tall stature.

Eickstedt, Riskey and Guha's delineation therefore, speak of eight or nine major elements in India's population. It is seen that a racial type with wavy hair, medium stature, thick protruded lips, broad bizygomatric arch and dark complexion described as Proto-Australoid by Guha, as Dravidian by Risley, as Pre-Dravidian by Haddon, as Veddid by Eickstedt and Nishada by Chanda stands as an important ethnic element in Central and Central Eastern India. Incidentally, this element also finds place in Indian epics. When we speak of racial elements in India, two important things merge. One of bracehycephalism and the other of earliest ethnic stratum. Regarding brachycephalism, Guha's views are accepted by other Anthropologists. The second aspect is the question of the earliest ethnic stratum. To this, some scholars feel that the earliest stratum was formed of pre-Dravidian element. Guha however contents that a Negrito element formed that earliest stratum. He has argued that the most primitive tribal communities such as Onge, Jarawas, Andamanese, Sentinelese are Negrito with frizzly/woolly hairs, prognathus face, dwarf stature and steatopygia among women. The Negrito substratum theory has been criticized by D N Majumdar and R P Chanda and others. These scholars argue that in case of India having earliest Negrito stratum, we should have found more Negrito skeletal remains from archaeological sites. However, there would have been more Negrito communities all over India.

CHAPTER – XII

Epilogue

In the previous paragraphs, we have followed the journey of Anthropology in India, in the yester years, from 1920 to 2020. The journey has been also to explore the culture of little known communities of the isolated pockets and to understand the process of cultural dynamics. The culture of the primitive communities who still retain the pristine quality in their culture, away from the busy urban or metropolitan areas, have always been the focus of Anthropology. Such isolated or less known groups have been studied to make theoretical formulations to accelerate the progress of Anthropology. During the last one hundred years, many Indian Universities have opened post graduate training and research in Anthropology to study villages and communities and to document varied social systems and processes of social transformation in different areas.

During all these past decades, there have been interaction among Anthropologists, between western and Indian scholars, between Anthropology and other branches of social sciences. As a result, the horizon of Anthropology has widened and there has been more acceptance of the views of different branches of social sciences. Some Anthropologists with their hardcore methodology have opted to stay in the settlements of the informant, for months, sharing native culture and thereby understanding the culture with objectivity. But some anthropologists have diluted their method and have emulated the strategy of other branches of social sciences.

We know that in different areas of our country, ethnographic studies have been undertaken by the researchers who have received cordial welcome from the people in the settlements in the far-flung areas. Anthropologists have spent months and months, in some cases, to collect ethnographic data in which the tribal and rural people have constructively collaborated. The present author still remembers the cordiality with which he and other members of his team have been greeted in Arunachal, Meghalaya, Manipur, Sikkim, Assam and Jharkhand. In Manipur the author has worked (along with a team) among the Purum Kuki tribe. It was a restudy and on the basis of this restudy (which was done by Anthropological Survey of India) a symposium was held in Calcutta in February 1983.(Details already stated in previous paragraphs). This community was earlier studied in 1936 by an eminent anthropologist TC Das (The results of the Symposium have been published in 1985). The present author (who was a senior editor of the Symposium volume) still feels the warmth of the Gallongs and of the Minyongs residing in the villages of Kabu and Pangin respectively in lower Siang valley of Arunachal. The same kind of good gesture has been enjoyed by the author in the Purum Kuki villages of Khongkhang and Tampak near the Myanmer border. It is sure that this kind of warmth and feeling of hospitality still exist and it is sure the people will still be eager to see the depiction of their culture- both etic view supported by people's emic view.

Today, question arises on what kind of study should be taken up? It is the author's feeling that cross cultural study, studies on change in economy and its impact, rise of different economic institutions, acceptance of technological innovations and its use, change in the family structure and coming up of new generations aspirations are some important dimensions that can be given priority and due importance in the future years. Along with these, the functional importance of different social institutions should also receive attention. When science predicts alarming dynamism in economy, in people's quality of life and in the attitude of people by 2050 AD, Anthropologists will have to be more aware to explore how and why traditional norms and values are becoming diluted and dysfunctional.

APPENDIX

Other publications by the same author

Sinha, Surajit, Biman Kumar Das Gupta and Hemendra Nath Banerjee, 1961. '*Agriculture,Crafts and Weekly Market of South Manbhum'*. Billetin of by Anthropological Survey of India, Vol. X , No.1.

Sinha, Surajit, Biman Kumar Das Gupta and Hemendra Nath Banerjee, 1966. '*Ethnic Groups,Village and Towns of Pargana Barabhum'*. Kolkata: Anthropological Survey of India, Memoir no. 14.

Lal, Parmanand and Biman Kumar Das Gupta, 1979. '*Lower Siang People*.' Kolkata : Anthropological Survey of India Memoir no. 50.

Das Gupta, Biman Kumar and Ajit K Danda (ed.), 1984. '*Tribal Education in India : in retrospect'*. Kolkata: Anthropological Survey of India, Memoir no. 61.

Das Gupta, Biman Kumar, Arabinda Basu, Bikash Raychaudhuri and Pabitra Gupta (edited), 1985. 'Proceedings of the Symposium on Purum (Chote) Revisited.' Kolkata: Anthropological Survey of India, Memoir no. 66.

Singh, K.S., Biman Das Gupta Tilak Bagchi and Pratima Chowdhury, 1993. '*Basketry in India' Material Traits Survey* : *Additional Data,* Kolkata: Anthropological Survey of India, Memoir no. 92.

Singh, K.S., Biman Das Gupta, Tilak Bagchi and Pratima Chowdhury, 1996. '*Occupation and Population in India' Material Traits Survey Additional data*', Kolkata: Anthropological Survey of India, Memoir no. 97.

Das Gupta, Biman Kumar. 2007. Anthropological Perspective, Kolkata.

Das Gupta, Biman Kumar, Jayanta Sarkar, Dipali Danda and Sumahan Bandyopadhyay 2014. '*Monasteries of Sikkim: Persistence of Cultural Tradition.*' Kolkata: Indian Anthropological Society.

Das Gupta, Biman Kumar, Samira Dasgupta and Amitabha Sarkar (editors), 2019. Retrospect of 100 yrs of Indian Anthropology, New Delhi: Aayu Publications..

Index

A

Abersing Kankung 62
achongpa 64
achumpihak 61
A.C. Mayer 19, 33
Adi-Dravida 23
Andamanese 80, 83, 90
Andaman Islanders 31
Andre Beteille 23, 26
Andrey Richards 38
Anthropological Atlas 47
Anthropological Survey of India 14, 16, 18, 19, 21, 23, 25, 27, 32, 34, 36, 43, 44, 45, 47, 49, 51, 57, 58, 59, 65, 67, 69, 70, 72, 87, 88, 92
Anthropologists 18, 30, 32, 33, 35, 38, 42, 45, 87, 89, 92, 93
Anthropology Club 15
Anthropos India 20
anti-liquor movement 54
Apatani 28, 37, 38, 81
Appico movement 54
A.R. Radcliffe Brown 31
AR Radcliffe Brown's 31
ataisey 68

B

Bhandarkar 18
Bhatra 52
Bhil 55, 80, 82
Bhoi Khasi 69
Bhotia 81, 82
Bhumij 52, 53, 67, 68, 80, 82
Bikash Roy Choudhury 15
bilineal 21, 80
Biraja Sankar Guha 88
Birhors 80
Birjia Culture 22
Bondo Highlanders 36, 37
Brahma Samaj Movement 53
Bronislaw Malinowski 30, 31, 33
B.S. Guha 13

C

Centre of Ecological Sciences 47

Chamedi 21
Charles de Ujfalvy 87
Chata parab 69
Chenchu 38, 83
Chipko movement 54
Cholanaicken 56
Chote 57, 58, 60, 61, 62, 63, 64, 65, 82
Choterim 61
Christopher Haimendorf 35
Christoph Haimendorf 39
Christoph Von Furer Haimendorf 37
cultural diversity 44
cultural dynamics 32, 58, 91
C.Von Eickstedt 87
C Von F Haimendorf 28

D

deyere 72
Dharani Sen 13
Dimasa 21, 80, 82
D N Majumdar 90
D.N. Majumdar 17
DN Majumdar 33, 42, 55
double descent 21
Drake Brockman 87

E

EB Tylor 31
Edward Jay 33
Elwin 16, 35, 36, 37, 42
endogenous methodology 18
endogenous methods 18
ET Dalton 31, 41, 52
ET Dalton's 41
ethnographic studies 31, 32, 42, 92
EVR Naicker 50, 51

F

F. G. Bailey 32
FLK Hsu 27
Franz Boas 29, 30

G

Gallong 72, 80, 81
Gallongs 92
Garo 69, 80, 82
Gauriya faith 73, 74
generalised exchange 13, 42, 57, 58, 62, 81
geographical classification 44
Ghatwal 68
Ghatwals 69
Ghotul 36
Gond 34, 36, 39, 42, 52, 80, 82
Gujjar 56

H

Haimendorf 28, 35, 37, 38, 39
haochongba 74
haorin 61
Haran Chandra Chakladar 13
Harry Verrier Holman Elwin 35
Herbert Risley's 88
Herbert Spencer 31
heterogeneous 85
HH Risley 31, 52
Hindu Samajer Garan 26
hiruhitongba 73
His Highness Namgyal 70
Hiyang 62
hloukal 61, 64
Ho 80, 82
hupal 64

I

I. Karve 32

Indian Anthropological Society 15, 20, 54
Indian Anthropology 18, 19, 25, 29, 32, 35
indigo revolt 54
Indira Gandhi 51
Ind parab 67
Ind Parab 69
inlok 64
Irawati Karve 18, 32

J

Jaddi 21
Jaintia 39, 69
Jaintia hills 39
Jarawas 80, 90
JH Hutton's 42
Jiro Yonokura 27
Journal of India Anthropological Society 20
Journal of Social Research 20
Juang 36, 80, 82
Jyotirao Govindrao Phule 50

K

Kacharis 22
Kharia 42, 52, 55
Khasi 22, 39, 42, 69, 70, 80, 81, 82
Khasi tribe 22
Khsatryisation 53
KL Sharma's 56
Koch 52, 71
Kolis 81
Koya 80, 83
K.P. Chattopadhyay 13, 16, 30, 31
KS Singh 46, 47, 51
KS Singh, 46
Kultur Kreise School 37
Kumar Suresh Singh 18, 32, 44, 45, 51

L

Lachen 70
Lachun 70
Laimren 61, 74, 75
Lalung 21, 22, 52, 82
Leiharaoba 74
Leiharoba 73
Lepcha 70, 82
Levi Strauss 57
L.K.A. Iyer 13
Loi Chakpa 73
Loi-Chakpa 52, 75, 76
London School of Economics 30, 38
loumi 64
LP Vidyarthi 42, 43

M

Mahatma Gandhi 35, 51
Maipak Yuhllung 62
Man-in-India' 15, 20
Mankids 80
Material Culture Traits 44
matrilineal 22, 30, 57, 80
matrilineal Khasis 22
Mckim Marriott 19, 33, 34, 43
Meitei 23, 61, 73, 74, 75, 76
Milton Singer 34
minhaba 80
Minyongs 81, 92
M.N. Srinivas 19, 50
MN Srinivas 33, 42, 43
Morris Opler 19, 32, 33
Munda 80, 81, 82
Mundas 42, 55

Myanmer border 93

N

nagadi 68
Nagas 55, 73, 81
Narayan Chandra Banerjee 13
National Informatics Centre 47
Nature-man- sprit complex 43
N Dutta Majumdar 42
NEFA 36, 37, 38
nichu 68
Nicobarese 81, 83
Nirmal Kumar Bose 13, 16, 18, 25, 32, 44, 49
N.K. Bose 32, 86
NK Bose 44, 45

O

Onge 80, 83, 90
Oraon 80, 81
Oscar Lewis 19, 32, 33

P

Pahira 52
pamlou 64
pan-Adivasi movement, 50
patrilineal 22, 57, 80
patrilineal Kacharis 22
Pemyangtse monastery 70
People of India 32, 45, 46, 77
Pipa 61
Pirring 62
Pnar Khasi 80
polyandry 71, 72, 81
preferential mating 58
PRT Gurdon 31, 42
PRT Gurdon's 42
Purum 13, 42, 57, 58, 59, 60, 61, 62, 63, 64, 65, 73, 81, 82, 92, 93
Purum Kuki 13, 42, 57, 81, 92, 93

Q

Queen Rani Gaidinliu 51

R

Rabari 81, 82
Rajbansi-Khastriya 71
Rajbansi- Khsatriya movement 53
Rajbansi Khsatriya Samity 71, 72
Ralph Nicholas 33, 34
Rama Prasad Chanda 13
Raymond Firth 38
R.K, Merton 31
Robert Redfield 34
Rodney Needham 57
Royal Anthropological Institute 30
Royal Asiatic Society 20
Royal Nepal Academy 39
R P Chanda 90
R.P. Chandra 18

S

Sadiyals 68, 69
Samajik Sanskritic Nribigyan 17
Sanamahi 61, 73, 74, 75
Sanamahi faith 73
Sanskritisation 43, 50, 53
Santal 52, 80, 81, 82
Sarat Chandra Roy 15, 16, 42, 55

Sardars 68, 69
saropa 64
Satya Sadhak Samaj 50, 51
school of Oriental African Studies 38
Sengfong 21
Sherpas 39
Shompen 80, 83
Siddi 82, 85
SN Navlakka 45
social mobility 43, 49, 52, 53, 71
Social mobility 53
Social Movement 53
social reformer 71
Sociologists 33, 42, 45
Surajit Chandra Sinha 15, 16, 19, 27, 33, 34, 43, 49, 51, 57

T

Taraf 68, 69
Tarak Chandra Das 13, 57
Tarak Chandra Roy Choudhury 15
Tarasis Mukherjee 34
tarpu 64
taukthipi 76
TB Naik's 55
TC Das 42, 57, 59, 60, 92
T.C. Ray Chaudhuri 13
Tebhaga 54
Thanthai Periyar 51
T.N. Madan 17
TN Pandit 56
Todas 81
transhumance 70, 71
Tribe- peasant- caste continuum 43
Trobraind Islanders 33
T.S. Epstein 20

U

Umonglei 74, 75

V

Veera Salinjam 50
Verrier Elwin 16, 35, 36, 37, 42

W

War Khasi 69
W H R Rivers 13
WHR Rivers 30, 31
W. Schmidt 37

1. Konayak Naga

2 (a) and 2 (b).Nagas with Traditional Attire

3. Digaru Mishmi Tribe of Arunachal Pradesh

4. Idu Mishmi Couple

5. Priest : Apatani Tribe, Arunachal Pradesh

6. Apatani Man

7. Khasi Tribe Meghalaya

8. Nocte Tribe of Manipur

9. Lushai (Mizo) Tribe , Mizoram

10. Garo Tribe

11. Former head hunter -Naga Tribe

12. Khemungan Naga, Nagaland

13. Apatani Woman at Zero Valley
(Courtesy : Personal collection from Pradeep Khisti for all photographs from 1 to 13 of north-east India)

14. Naga Woman in Traditional Attire

15. Naga Dance

16. Wancho and Nocte in Dancing Attire

17. Ao Naga